W9-COX-147

What Happens When
Volcanoes Erupt?

138939

What Happens When
Volcanoes
Erupt?

Daphne Butler

RSVP
RAINTREE
STECK-VAUGHN
PUBLISHERS
The Steck-Vaughn Company

Austin, Texas

© Copyright 1996, text, Steck-Vaughn Company

All rights reserved. No part of this book may be reproduced or utilized in any form or by any means, electronic or mechanical, including photocopying, recording, or by any information storage and retrieval system, without permission in writing from the Publisher. Inquiries should be addressed to: Copyright Permissions, Steck-Vaughn Company, P.O. Box 26015, Austin, TX 78755

Published by Raintree Steck-Vaughn Publishers, an imprint of Steck-Vaughn Company

Library of Congress Cataloging-in-Publication Data

Butler, Daphne, 1945–
    What happens when volcanoes erupt? / Daphne Butler.
        p.   cm. — (What happens when—?)
    Includes index.
    ISBN 0-8172-4157-4
    1. Volcanoes—Juvenile literature. [1. Volcanoes.]   I. Title.
    II. Series: Butler, Daphne, 1945–   What happens when—?
    QE521.3.B87   1996
    551.2'1—dc20   95-10519
                                                                   CIP
                                                                    AC

Printed and bound in Singapore
1 2 3 4 5 6 7 8 9 0 99 98 97 96 95

Contents

Once Long, Long Ago

Long ago, when the Earth was a new planet, it was very different.

It was not a good place to live. There were no animals, plants, or trees.
It was just dry and dead.

Boiling Rock

Even so, the Earth was not still.
Under its thin **crust**, boiling rock was
stirring around.

Often the boiling rock would break
through the crust and pour out across
the land.

Property of
Bayport - Blue Point Public Library

Millions of Years

Millions of years went by. The land became more solid. Rain fell and made the oceans. The rain broke up the rocks, and soil formed.

The soil was rich. Life began. It was a very long time before the world came to look the way it does today.

11

There are still places in the world where mountains suddenly explode. Dust, gas, and liquid rock pour out over the land.

We call the liquid rock **lava**. We call the mountains volcanoes. People study volcanoes so that they can learn more about the Earth.

Living with Volcanoes

People who live near volcanoes can never be sure of what will happen. Sometimes there are **earthquakes** as the rocks shift and settle.

Sometimes dust and **ash** burst into the air. The dust settles on houses and buries them.

Volcano scientists try to warn people when to leave their homes. If they stay, they, too, will be buried.

Flowing Lava

Lava flows down mountains in rivers. It finds the easiest and fastest way to travel.

When it cools, it moves more slowly. Later, it will become solid rock.

Cone Shapes

Each time a volcano **erupts**, it grows higher. It forms in the shape of a cone. Old volcanoes are beautiful because of their perfect shape.

On top, there is a valley called a
crater. Here holes may lead to the
inside of the volcano. Sometimes the
crater smokes from the heat.

19

Inside a Crater

The inside of a crater can be a dangerous place.

The sides are steep, and the ground is hot. There are smelly fumes and sometimes lakes of fresh lava.

Aging Volcanoes

When the rocks become steadier, volcanoes stop erupting. The land cools. The rocks break up, and plants start to grow.

There may be lakes of hot water, where the water sprays high up into the air.

The volcanoes appear to be long dead, but they might erupt again!

Using the Heat

Long after volcanoes have stopped erupting, the rocks below the ground are still very hot.

Water comes steaming up to the surface. In some places, it is piped to nearby towns. Once there, the water is used for heating.

In other places, natural steam is used to make electricity.

Good Farmland

One reason why people live near volcanoes is because the land is so good for growing crops.

When the land is covered by volcanic dust or lava, plants are buried or burned by the heat. But once the land has been broken up, it makes very good farmland.

27

Volcano Words

ash Bits of lava, rock, and dust that some volcanoes spray into the air

crater An opening in the top of a volcano made by an explosion

crust The hard outer surface that covers the Earth

earthquake

A time when the ground shakes. It happens when rocks under the land or ocean begin to move.

erupts Explodes or forces out

lava Liquid rock that flows out of a volcano. It slowly cools down and then becomes solid.

Index

M
mountains 12, 13, 17

P
people 13, 14, 15, 26
plants 6, 22, 27

R
rain 10
rocks 9, 10, 12, 14, 17,
    22, 25

S
scientists 15
soil 10, 11

T
trees 6

Globe Enterprises © 1993
Published in association with Macdonald Young Books Ltd